TECHNOLOGY TOPICS
SPACE
Steve Blackman
illustrated by **Nick Shrewing**
photography by **Martyn Chillmaid**

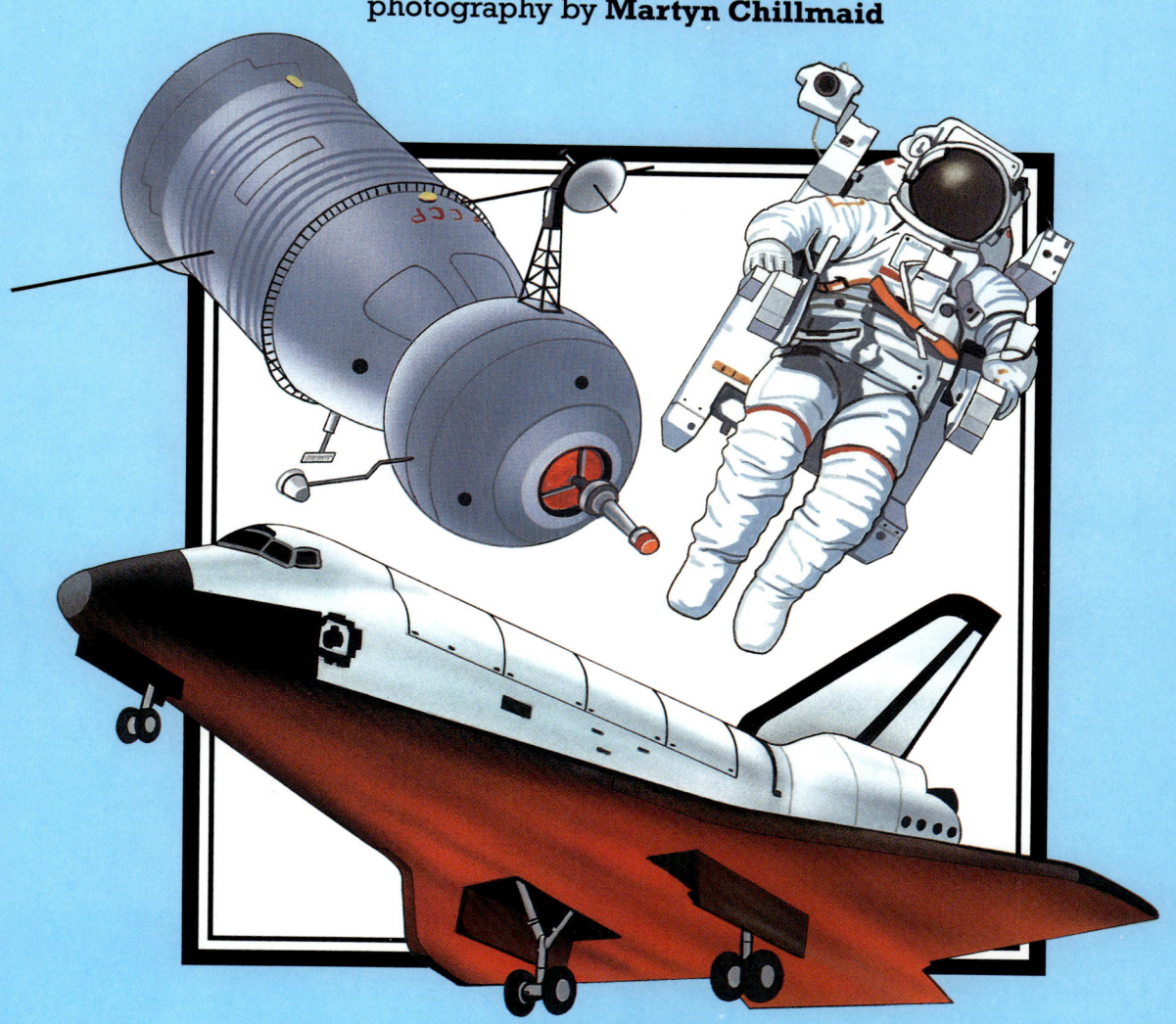

WATTS BOOKS
London ▪ New York ▪ Sydney

© Watts Books 1993

Watts Books
96 Leonard Street
London
EC2A 4RH

Franklin Watts Australia
14 Mars Road
Lane Cove
NSW 2066

UK ISBN: 0 7496 1327 0
10 9 8 7 6 5 4 3 2 1
Dewey Decimal Classification 629.4

Series Editor: Hazel Poole
Editor: Chris Oxlade
Designer: Glynn Pickerill
Illustrator: Nick Shrewing
Cover design and artwork: Mike Davis
Design Production: The R & B Partnership
Photography: Martyn Chillmaid
Consultant: Rowland Penfold

A CIP catalogue record for this book is available from the British Library

Printed in the United Kingdom

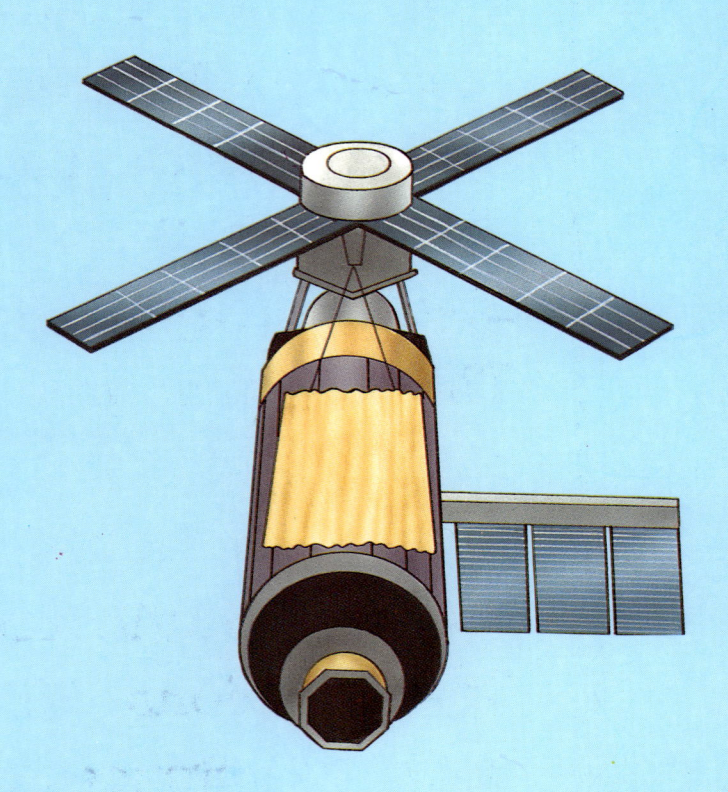

CONTENTS

Space Craft 4

Spacecraft Toys 6

Probes and Unmanned Spacecraft 8

Building a Space Probe 10

The Moon Programme 12

Moon Town 14

The Space Shuttle 16

A Space Shuttle Model 18

Space Stations 20

Building a Space Station 22

Space Travellers 24

Is Anybody Out There? 26

Space Travel Through
  The Ages 28

Glossary 30

Resources 31

Index 32

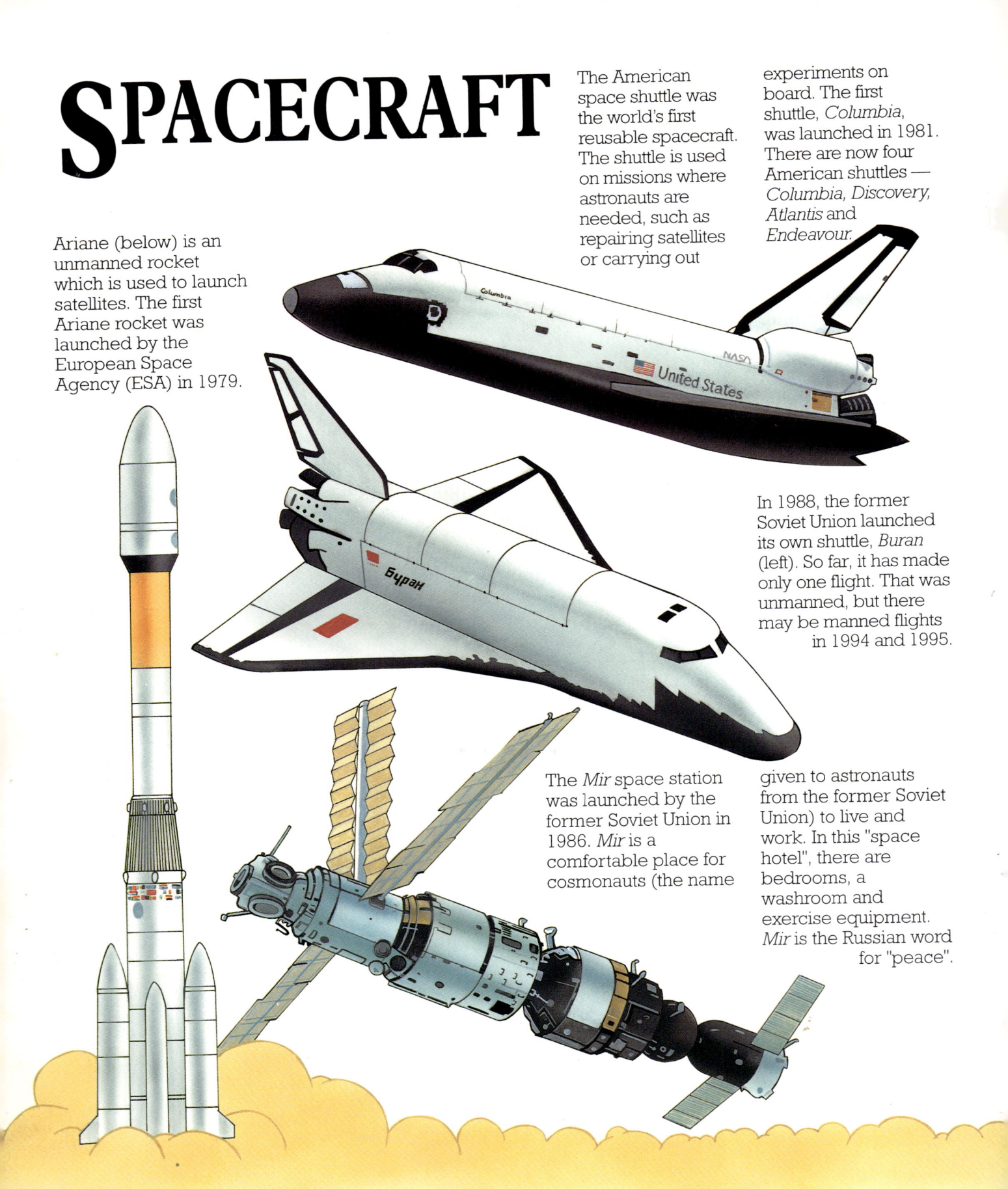

SPACECRAFT

Ariane (below) is an unmanned rocket which is used to launch satellites. The first Ariane rocket was launched by the European Space Agency (ESA) in 1979.

The American space shuttle was the world's first reusable spacecraft. The shuttle is used on missions where astronauts are needed, such as repairing satellites or carrying out experiments on board. The first shuttle, *Columbia*, was launched in 1981. There are now four American shuttles — *Columbia, Discovery, Atlantis* and *Endeavour*.

In 1988, the former Soviet Union launched its own shuttle, *Buran* (left). So far, it has made only one flight. That was unmanned, but there may be manned flights in 1994 and 1995.

The *Mir* space station was launched by the former Soviet Union in 1986. *Mir* is a comfortable place for cosmonauts (the name given to astronauts from the former Soviet Union) to live and work. In this "space hotel", there are bedrooms, a washroom and exercise equipment. *Mir* is the Russian word for "peace".

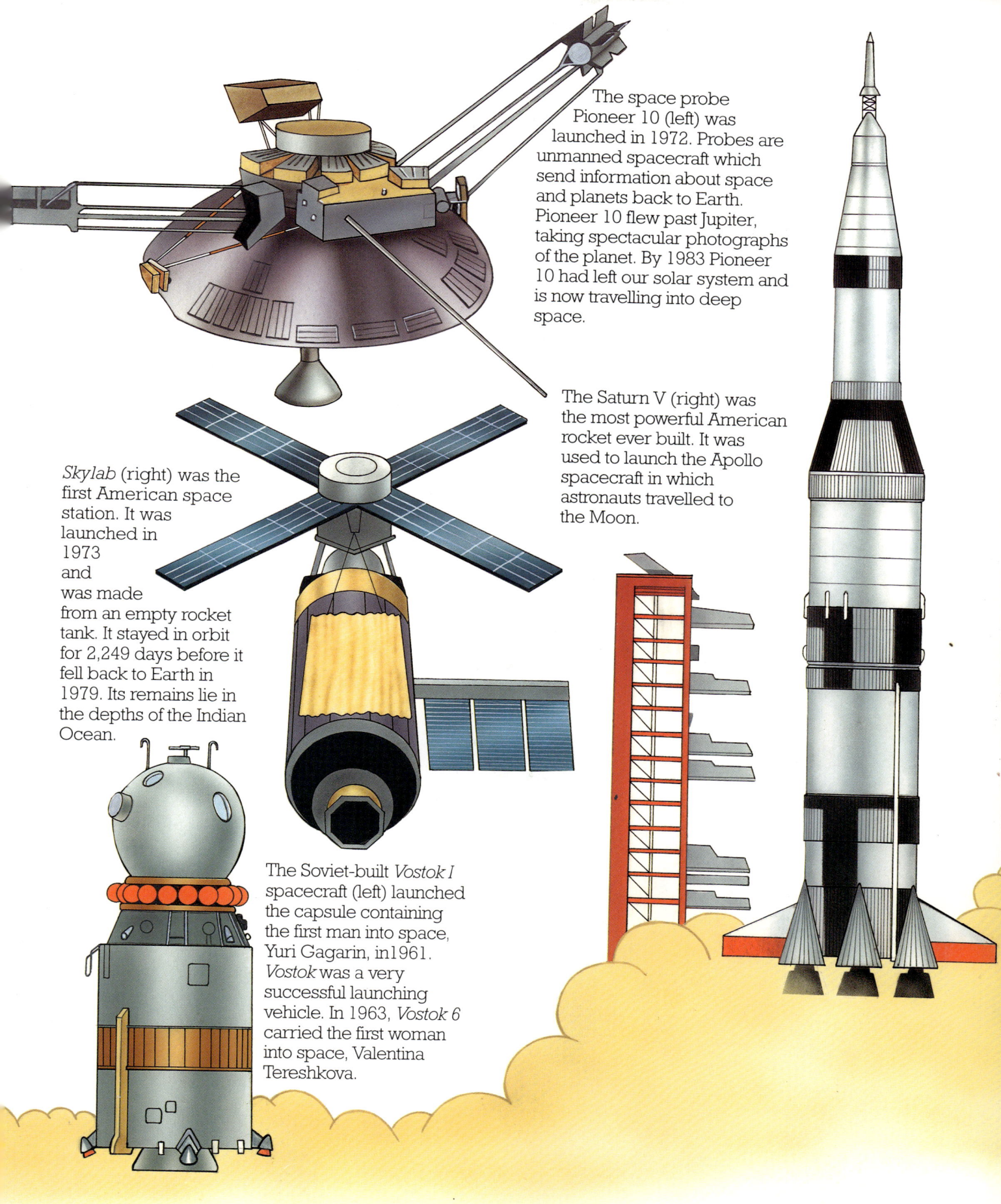

The space probe Pioneer 10 (left) was launched in 1972. Probes are unmanned spacecraft which send information about space and planets back to Earth. Pioneer 10 flew past Jupiter, taking spectacular photographs of the planet. By 1983 Pioneer 10 had left our solar system and is now travelling into deep space.

The Saturn V (right) was the most powerful American rocket ever built. It was used to launch the Apollo spacecraft in which astronauts travelled to the Moon.

Skylab (right) was the first American space station. It was launched in 1973 and was made from an empty rocket tank. It stayed in orbit for 2,249 days before it fell back to Earth in 1979. Its remains lie in the depths of the Indian Ocean.

The Soviet-built *Vostok I* spacecraft (left) launched the capsule containing the first man into space, Yuri Gagarin, in 1961. *Vostok* was a very successful launching vehicle. In 1963, *Vostok 6* carried the first woman into space, Valentina Tereshkova.

SPACECRAFT TOYS

Making a spacecraft toy is a good way to think about what shape a rocket should be. Rockets need to travel extremely fast to get into orbit around the Earth. *Vostok 1* reached 28,260 km/h. To reach space, a rocket has to travel up through the Earth's atmosphere. The air tries to slow down the rocket, so the rocket needs to be a streamlined shape.

To make a toy spacecraft
You may need:

- a large plastic drinks bottle
- white paper
- thin card
- paints
- felt
- needle and cotton
- scissors
- glue

1 A plastic drinks bottle makes a good base for a rocket model. Choose the most streamlined bottle you have. Make a cone using thin card and fix it to the top of the bottle. Cover the bottle and cone with strips of white paper. Try to get the paper as smooth as possible.

2 The tail fins of a rocket make it stable and stop it spinning round as it flies along. Make your tail fins from card. Decide how many you need and what shape they should be. Carefully glue them into place.

3 Many rockets are metal coloured. Why not paint yours with different colours?

4 Finish your model by making small badges and logos for it. You could design them around your name, or your town or country.

Why not make a soft spacecraft toy for a very young child? Flying saucer shapes are easy to make using coloured felt.

Remember: the toys you have made could be used by children younger than yourself. So make sure that there are no small pieces that could easily fall off.

7

PROBES and unmanned SPACECRAFT

Manned missions into space usually make headline news, but unmanned missions are just as important. Unmanned space probes help us to learn about our solar system. Probes have flown past all the planets except Pluto, and landed on some of them. Some of the missions have taken many years.

Planets and probes

Planet	1st probe to visit		1st probe to land	
Moon	Luna 3	1959	Luna 9	1966
Mercury	Mariner 10	1974		
Venus	Mariner 2	1962	Venera 7	1970
Mars	Mariner 4	1965	Viking 1	1976
Jupiter	Pioneer 10	1973		
Saturn	Pioneer 11	1979		
Uranus	Voyager 2	1986		
Neptune	Voyager 2	1989		
Pluto	Planned for the early 21st century			

Viking 1 and 2

These two American probes were launched in 1975 to land on Mars. Two were sent in case one broke down. Both landed to search for signs of life, but they found nothing. The Viking probes carried instruments for recording the Mars weather. The winds were very light, but it was freezing cold – from -80°C to -150°C.

ROBOTIC CAMERAS sent back pictures to Earth, giving scientists their best view yet of the "Red Planet".

Voyager 1 and 2

Both Voyager probes were launched by the United States in 1977. They flew past Jupiter and took spectacular pictures of the famous Great Red Spot.

The probes then flew to Saturn and took photographs of its rings. Voyager 1 took more photographs of Titan, one of Saturn's moons.

From Saturn, Voyager 2 flew to the distant planets of Uranus and Neptune. It took 12 years to reach Neptune, where it measured winds of just over 1000 km/h and found six new moons. Voyager 2 is still travelling through space. On board is a gold-plated record which shows what life on Earth is like, just in case it is found by other beings.

Giotto

The probe Giotto was sent by the European Space Agency (ESA) to photograph Halley's comet when it came close to the Earth in 1986. Giotto took the first photographs of the comet's centre, which is made of ice and rock.

Where to next?

Space probes which landed on the Moon sent us lots of information which was used to plan the manned Moon landings. Perhaps one day space probes will find another planet that can support life, just like the Earth.

Building a Space Probe

Space probes can be launched by rocket or by reusable shuttle. The probe is sent off into space at just the right speed and direction so that it travels close to the planet it is going to explore. Probes do not carry much fuel and they only have small engines to make tiny changes to their course.

To make a model space probe

You may need:
- **aluminium foil (different colours)**
- **card tubes**
- **wire**
- **straws**
- **card**
- **glue**
- **scissors**
- **paint**
- **wood**
- **small lids and cartons**

1 Look closely at the different space probe pictures. Study how the probes are made. Remember that because they are travelling through space they do not need to be very strong. Make an interesting shaped frame for your probe. You could use straws, strips of wood or wire. Paint the frame with silver or gold paint.

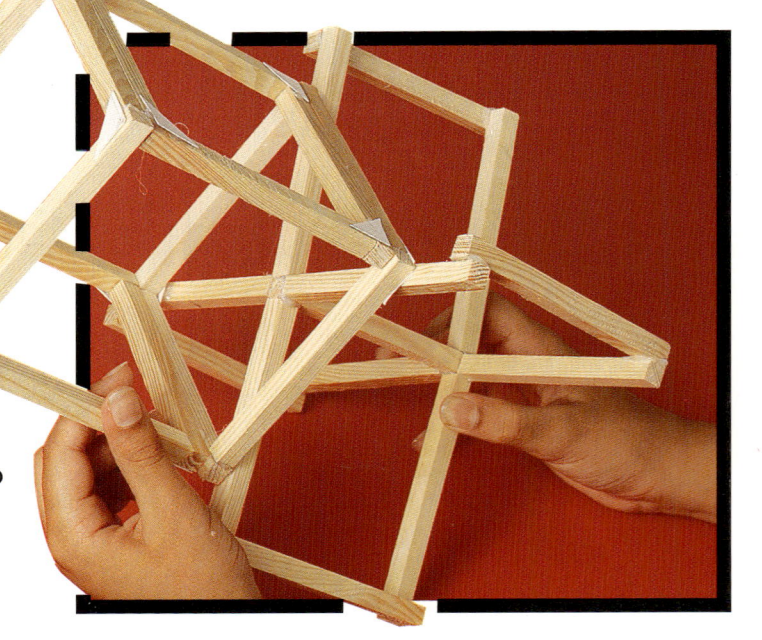

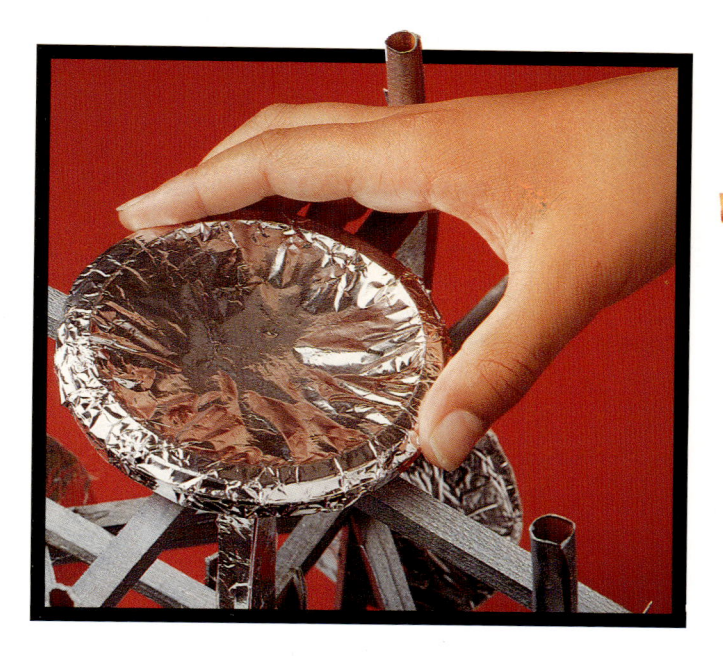

2 Your probe will need a radio dish for sending photographs and information back to Earth. One way of making this is to cover a lid with aluminium foil.

3 Voyager has 16 tiny rockets which are used to change its course. Think about where you could put small rockets and how they would change the probe's course. You could make the rockets from small rolls of thin card.

4 Real probes have lots of detectors, sensors, cameras and other instruments. You could use different shaped lids, matchboxes and wires for your instruments. Cover them with coloured foil.

Can you work out a way to attach small light bulbs and a battery to your probe?

Try to make some of the foil reflect the lights.

A rubbish dump in outer space

What do you think happens to space probes and satellites when they wear out or break down? The answer is simple – they become space junk! Over 5,000 probes and satellites have been launched. Some of them fall back to Earth in the end and burn up in the atmosphere. But many are still floating about. Scientists are worried that space junk could be a danger to future space travellers.

11

The Moon Programme

The Race for the Moon

In May 1961, President John F Kennedy started the race to the Moon. He promised that the United States would land a man on the Moon and return him safely to Earth before the decade was over.

During the 1960s excitement grew as the United States and the former Soviet Union competed in the "space race". In 1965 men from both countries made space walks outside their spacecraft – first a Soviet cosmonaut and then an American astronaut.

In 1968 the American spacecraft Apollo 8 orbited around the Moon. The astronauts sent back live television pictures to Earth. On 16 July 1969, America launched the Saturn V rocket carrying Apollo 11. On board were astronauts Neil Armstrong, Edwin Aldrin and Michael Collins. On 20 July, millions of people watched live television pictures as Neil Armstrong climbed down the ladder from the lunar module onto the surface of the Moon.

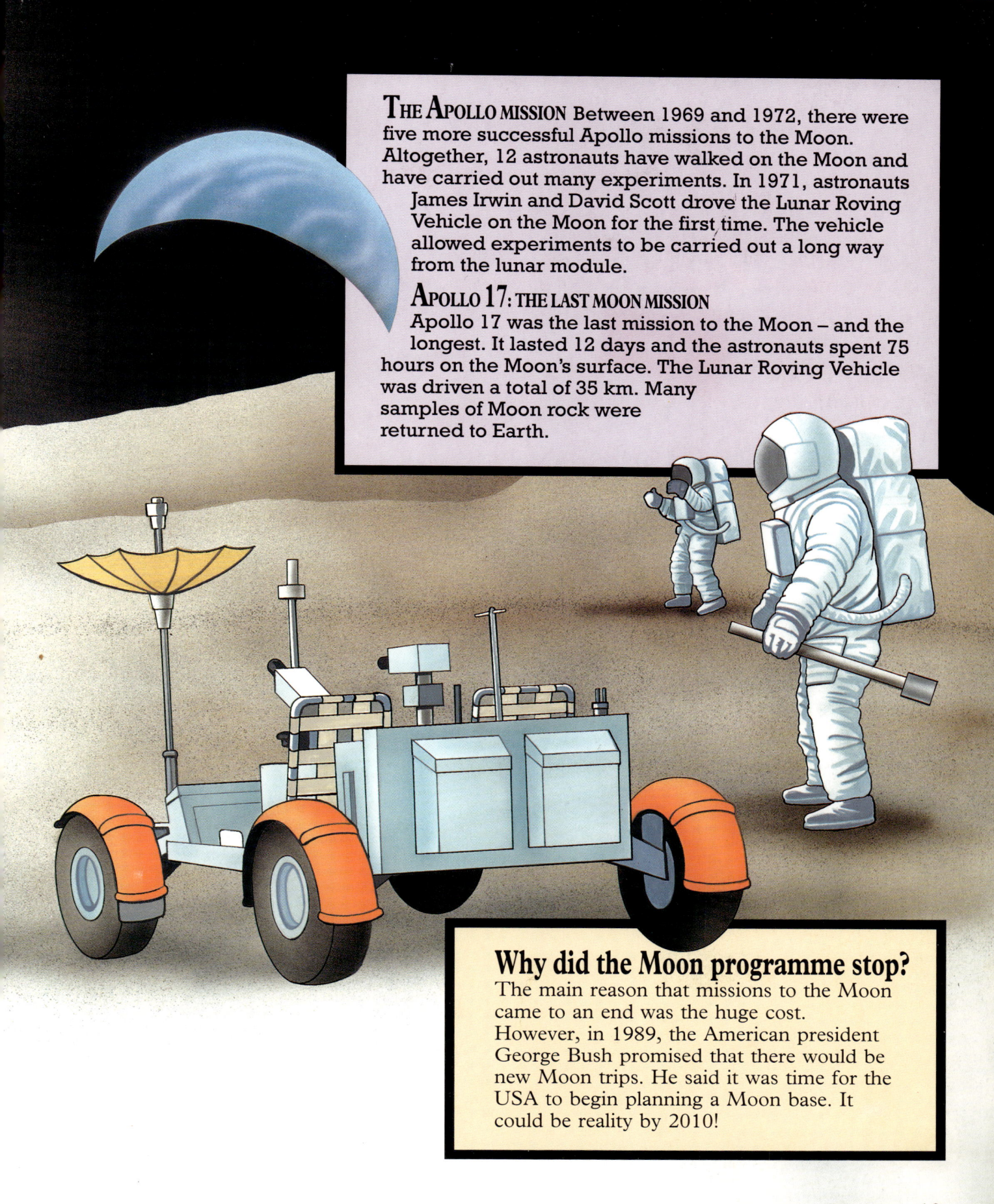

THE APOLLO MISSION Between 1969 and 1972, there were five more successful Apollo missions to the Moon. Altogether, 12 astronauts have walked on the Moon and have carried out many experiments. In 1971, astronauts James Irwin and David Scott drove the Lunar Roving Vehicle on the Moon for the first time. The vehicle allowed experiments to be carried out a long way from the lunar module.

APOLLO 17: THE LAST MOON MISSION
Apollo 17 was the last mission to the Moon – and the longest. It lasted 12 days and the astronauts spent 75 hours on the Moon's surface. The Lunar Roving Vehicle was driven a total of 35 km. Many samples of Moon rock were returned to Earth.

Why did the Moon programme stop?

The main reason that missions to the Moon came to an end was the huge cost. However, in 1989, the American president George Bush promised that there would be new Moon trips. He said it was time for the USA to begin planning a Moon base. It could be reality by 2010!

Moon Town

Many science-fiction film makers and authors have tried to imagine what a Moon base will look like. The announcement that there could be a real Moon base in the early part of the next century could turn science fiction into fact!

Planning a Moon town

If you were in charge of planning the first Moon settlement, where would you build it? Would it be in a crater? Or near mountains or on the flat plains?

What materials would you use for the buildings? Remember that there is only rock and dust on the Moon!

Who would actually construct the buildings?

To build a model Moon town
You may need:

- a baseboard
- chicken wire
- egg boxes
- paints
- polystyrene packing
- card tubes
- small cartons
- newspaper
- wallpaper paste (fungicide free)
- glue

1 Draw some plans of the Moon town you want to build. As you do, think about the materials you will use and the size of the model.

2 Find a baseboard for your model. It could be plywood, hardboard, chipboard or thick card. A board about 70 cm square is ideal. Anything bigger will be difficult to manage.

3 Use chicken wire to build up a landscape of hills, valleys and large craters. Cover this with papier mâché. You can mould the papier mâché into smaller craters and hills. Don't make the papier mâché too thick or it will take a long time to dry out.

4 Allow plenty of time for the papier mâché to dry out before you paint it. Use darker colours inside the craters.

5 It is possible that the first Moon buildings will be made from empty rocket cases. Make these using card tubes and glue them into place.

How many shelters are you going to include?
How will people move between them?
Will there be offices, workshops and laboratories?
Will people wear space suits or will there be an air supply inside every building?

6 Imagine that you have to extend the first Moon town into a community of about 1000 people. Include your ideas on your model.

Where will you get water from?
Where will you get oxygen from?
How will you get rid of waste?
Who will live in your Moon town and how will you choose them?

What will the real Moon town look like?

The answer is that nobody really knows! It may be a collection of cylindrical buildings which are partly underground. Some scientists believe that Moon dust could be mixed with other materials to make a form of concrete for buildings. Others think that oxygen could be found in Moon rock.

15

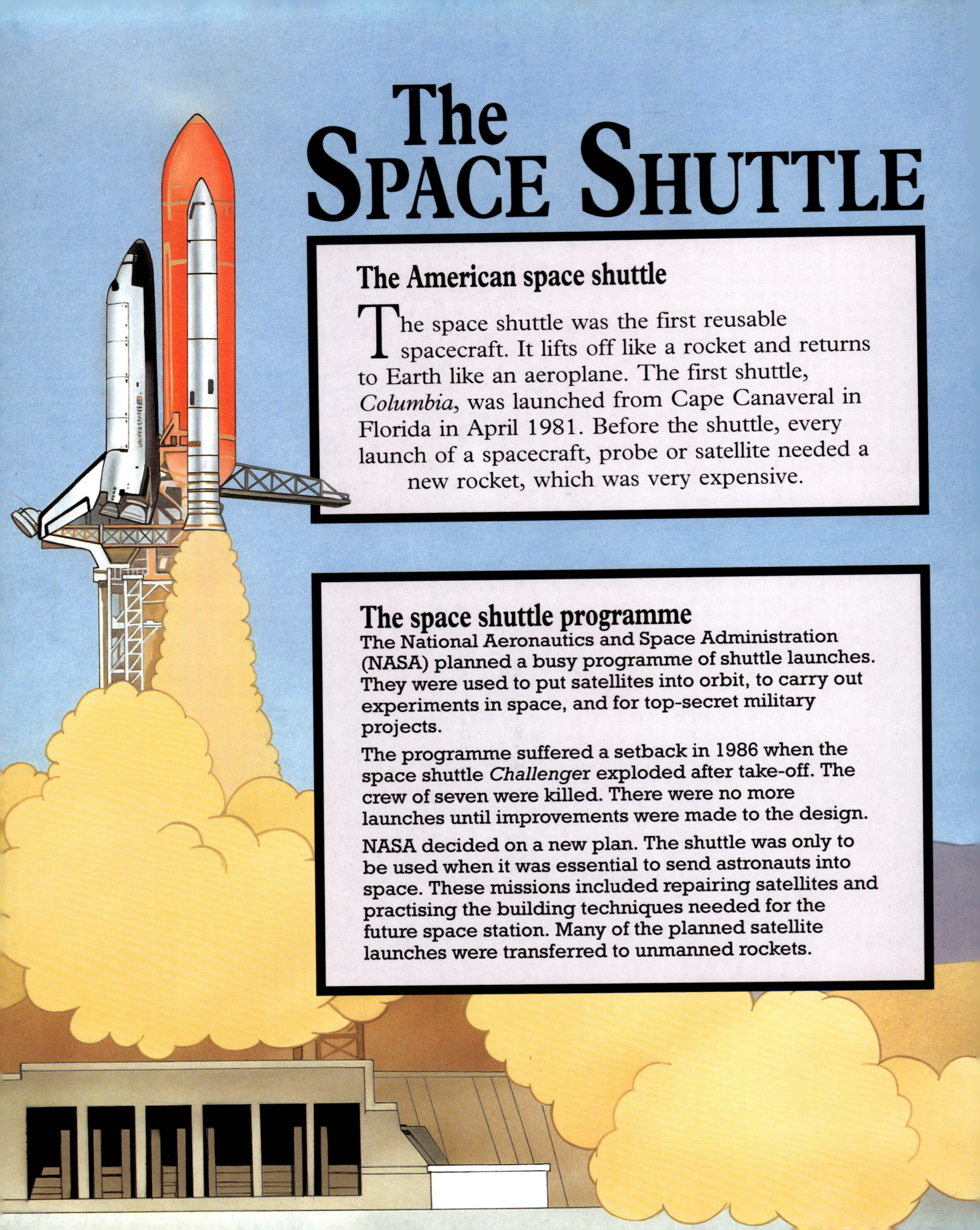

The Space Shuttle

The American space shuttle

The space shuttle was the first reusable spacecraft. It lifts off like a rocket and returns to Earth like an aeroplane. The first shuttle, *Columbia*, was launched from Cape Canaveral in Florida in April 1981. Before the shuttle, every launch of a spacecraft, probe or satellite needed a new rocket, which was very expensive.

The space shuttle programme

The National Aeronautics and Space Administration (NASA) planned a busy programme of shuttle launches. They were used to put satellites into orbit, to carry out experiments in space, and for top-secret military projects.

The programme suffered a setback in 1986 when the space shuttle *Challenger* exploded after take-off. The crew of seven were killed. There were no more launches until improvements were made to the design.

NASA decided on a new plan. The shuttle was only to be used when it was essential to send astronauts into space. These missions included repairing satellites and practising the building techniques needed for the future space station. Many of the planned satellite launches were transferred to unmanned rockets.

The crew of the space shuttle *Columbia*

LAUNCHING THE SHUTTLE
For launch, the shuttle is connected to a huge fuel tank and two rocket boosters. The tank carries fuel for the shuttle's engines. The boosters have their own fuel and give the thrust needed for launch.

Two minutes after launch the booster rockets separate from the shuttle and parachute into the ocean. They are collected and re-used.

After eight minutes the main engines shut down and the fuel tank separates. The tank burns up as it falls to Earth. Two smaller engines fire to accelerate the shuttle to its orbiting speed of 28,000 km/h. It is now 250 km above the Earth.

RETURN TO EARTH
At the end of its mission, the shuttle is turned around and special engines are fired. This slows it down and it begins to drop back to Earth. As the shuttle re-enters the Earth's atmosphere, friction with the air heats up the underneath, making it glow red hot. The shuttle gradually slows down and then glides to its runway, where it lands like an aeroplane.

THE CREW
There are normally five people in a shuttle crew. They are the flight commander, a pilot, and three specialists, who are usually scientists. Crew members spend years training for a flight. They also need to be reasonably fit.

Crews practise for their missions in simulated zero gravity because in space everything becomes weightless. Eating and drinking needs special care because liquids float around in large drops. Space food is now much better than it used to be — astronauts can now choose from about 90 items, including scrambled egg and real bread.

A Space Shuttle Model

What does the shuttle look like?

The space shuttle is a winged spacecraft. Between the cockpit and the engines is a large cargo bay. Two cargo bay doors on the top of the fuselage open when the shuttle is in orbit. There are powerful engines at the rear, and the tail and wings have flaps which are used to control the shuttle as it lands. About 31,000 special black and white tiles protect the shuttle from the immense heat as it flies back into the Earth's atmosphere. The tiles fit together like a huge jigsaw.

To make a Space Shuttle
You may need:
- a rectangular plastic bottle
- thin card
- white paper
- paint
- glue
- scissors
- felt pens or crayons

1 Study pictures of the shuttle. Look at the shape and colour, and the details on its surface.

2 Cut a wing shape from paper and use it as a template to make two card wings. Glue the wings onto the underside of a rectangular plastic bottle. Cut another piece of card for the tail fin. You will need to cut some flaps at the bottom of the tail so that you can glue it onto the bottle.

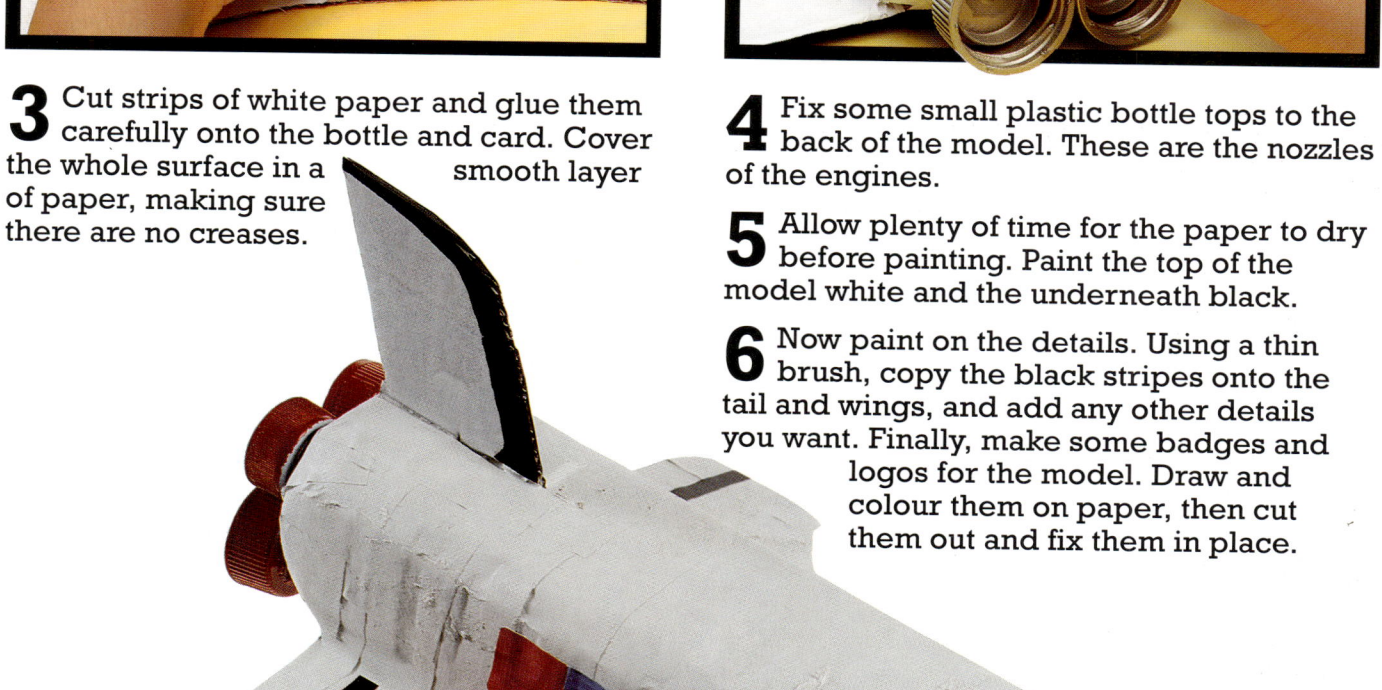

3 Cut strips of white paper and glue them carefully onto the bottle and card. Cover the whole surface in a smooth layer of paper, making sure there are no creases.

4 Fix some small plastic bottle tops to the back of the model. These are the nozzles of the engines.

5 Allow plenty of time for the paper to dry before painting. Paint the top of the model white and the underneath black.

6 Now paint on the details. Using a thin brush, copy the black stripes onto the tail and wings, and add any other details you want. Finally, make some badges and logos for the model. Draw and colour them on paper, then cut them out and fix them in place.

Did you know ...
Every space shuttle mission has a specially designed badge. The badge includes a picture of the shuttle, the names of the crew and some symbols for the mission.

Look at the pictures on pages 16 and 17 of the shuttle landing after a mission. Now try to design and make an undercarriage for your model.

Can you make the wheels go round? Can you make the undercarriage rectractable?

19

Space Stations

The first space station was launched by the former Soviet Union in 1971. It was called *Salyut 1* and inside was a work area, a compartment for resting and a treadmill for the cosmonauts to use to keep fit.

The idea of the space station was to provide a place where tests and experiments could be carried out. The cosmonauts themselves were also under test – to see how long people could live in space.

Seven Salyut space stations were launched altoghter. Each time lessons were learnt and the next station was improved. In 1986, the Soviets launched the *Mir* space station. It has been occupied by cosmonauts ever since.

SKYLAB, the first American space station, was launched in 1973. *Skylab* was more comfortable than *Salyut*. The astronauts had more room to work, and even had a shower and a proper toilet. *Skylab* was used until February 1974.

There were three missions to *Skylab*. Each time an Apollo spacecraft was launched with a Saturn 1B rocket and docked with the space station. The first mission lasted 28 days, the second for 59 days and the third for 84 days. The missions proved that humans could stay in space for long periods of time without suffering too many ill effects.

How is a space station powered?

Salyut and *Skylab* both got their energy from the Sun. Once they were in orbit, large solar panels unfolded. These turned light from the Sun into electricity for the space station. The *Skylab* mission almost failed because one of the solar panels was damaged during the launch. Astronauts had to make a dangerous space walk to mend it.

Space station Freedom

In 1984, President Ronald Reagan made the exciting announcement that the biggest space station yet was to be built. It was soon named *Freedom*, and was to be an international effort between the United States, Canada, Japan and some European countries, including Britain.

Freedom will be a laboratory and an environmental observatory, used to study the Earth and space. Space planes are being designed which will ferry astronauts to and from the station. One space plane, called *Hermes*, is being designed by the European Space Agency (ESA).

NASA plans to start building *Freedom* in 1995. It will probably take 25 space shuttle missions to carry all the parts for the station into space. *Freedom* should be finished around the year 2000. At first, astronauts will spend about three months at a time working there. Eventually up to eight astronauts will live on the station, staying for six months.

Building a Space Station

Space stations are assembled in zero gravity. This has many advantages compared to building on Earth. The structure can be very light and flimsy and the different parts are easy to move into place. But there are disadvantages too. On Earth, you use your weight to turn a spanner. In space you have no weight, so tightening a bolt is hard work. Working in a bulky space-suit is also tricky.

To build a space station model

You may need:

- art straws
- aluminium foil
- card tubes
- thin wire
- paints
- small cartons
- glue
- fishing line
- card
- string
- pipe cleaners

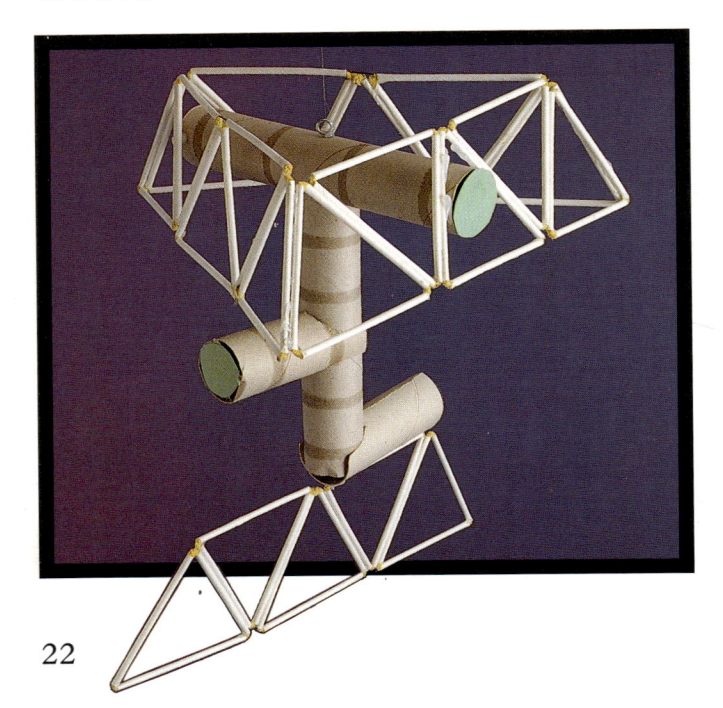

1 A space station model can be based on a frame of art straws and wire. Before you begin, make some drawings to work out the shape you want. Avoid having bends in the frame.

2 Build the frame from art straws and wire. Make joints using pipe cleaners pushed into the ends of the straws.

3 Decide what shape and size your living quarters and laboratories will be. Card tubes with covered ends are good for these.

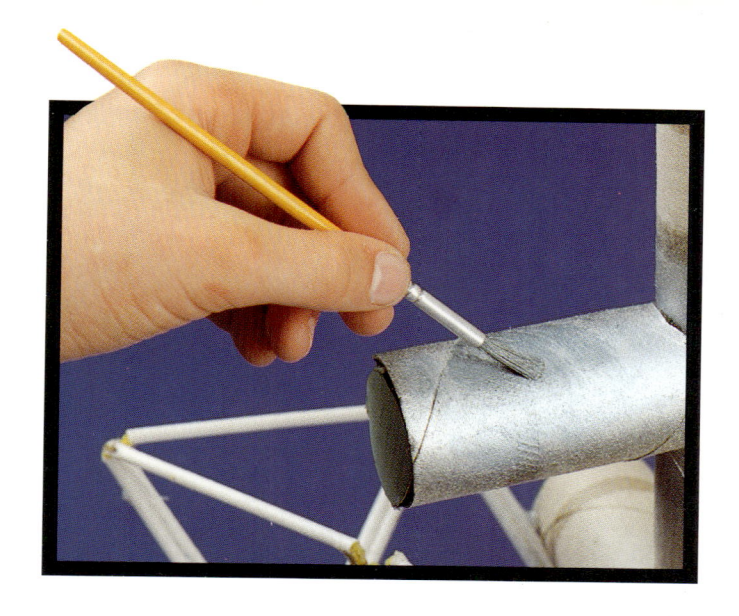

4 This is a good time to paint the model. It's best to use gold or silver spray paint, but painting with a brush will also work. Be careful with spray paints.

5 Make solar panels from small pieces of card covered with gold or silver foil. Glue them onto the frame. Think about which way they should point.

Space plane

You know that the European Space Agency is planning a space plane to travel between Earth and the Freedom space station. Try to design your own space plane. It will need to carry eight passengers and some cargo. Think about how it will take off and land. What sort of engines will it have? Why not make it at the same scale as your space station?

6 Think about the best way to display your model. You could hang it from the ceiling in your room. It would be fun to shine lights onto the solar panels in the dark.

THE WORLD IN SPACE

Space Travellers

Astronauts and cosmonauts from more than 25 different countries have gone into space. Most of them have travelled on Soviet spacecraft to the *Salyut* and *Mir* space stations. Many others have flown in the space shuttle. The first person from the United Kingdom to go into space was Helen Sharman in 1991. She was chosen from 12,000 applicants to become a cosmonaut and travel in a *Soyuz* spacecraft to the *Mir* space station, where she stayed for eight days.

Countries in space

Apart from the United States, the former Soviet Union and Europe, there are several other countries who are playing a role in space. Most of them have launched unmanned rockets with satellites on board.

India

India has successfully launched communication satellites. People in remote villages in India can make telephone calls and receive television broadcasts via the satellites.

In 1984, an Indian cosmonaut flew to the *Salyut* space station. He was part of the crew on board the Soviet *Soyuz T11* mission.

Israel

In 1988, Israel became the eighth country to launch a satellite with its own rocket. The rocket was called Shavit, which means "Comet", and the satellite was called Offeq, which means "Horizon". Israel launched a second satellite in 1990.

China
By the end of 1990, China had successfully launched 33 satellites. The Chinese are now planning a manned space programme, but its details are top secret. Chinese rockets are known as Cheng Zen, which means "Long March". The Chinese sell space on their rockets to other countries who want to send satellites into orbit.

Japan
The Japanese launched a satellite in 1970. They were the fourth country to do so. There are two rocket launching sites in Japan, but they only operate for a few months each year. Japanese space scientists have great plans for the future, including a reusable space plane.

Long-distance space travel
When it is in orbit, the space shuttle travels at 28,000 km/h. It goes around the Earth every 90 minutes! That seems very fast, but its far too slow for travelling around our own solar system. To travel to the nearest star (apart from the Sun) would take over 150,000 years! Even a spacecraft which could travel at the speed of light (300,000 km/second) would take four years to make the journey.

Imagine spending four years inside a tiny spacecraft. How would the crew keep healthy? What would they eat. What would they do to keep from getting bored? What about collisions with asteroids?

For the moment long-distance space travel is for science-fiction films only.

Is Anybody Out There

The *Pioneer* message

The space probe *Pioneer 10* was launched in 1972. It reached Jupiter in 1973 and is now travelling into deep space. On board is a special plaque. On the plaque is a diagram designed to tell intelligent beings about Earth and our solar system.

The Voyager message

The *Voyager* probes were launched in 1977. On board is a special gold-plated record (the compact disc had not yet been invented in 1977). On the record are examples of music from around the world, greetings in 60 languages and the sounds of birds and animals. The idea was devised by the American astronomer Carl Sagan.

To make a space capsule

You may need:

- a container with a lid (a dried milk tin is ideal)
- paint
- crayons
- felt pens
- paper

JUPITER and two of its moons, photographed by *Voyager 1* space probe in 1979.

1. Decide what sort of information you want to send into outer space and make a list. Here are some ideas:

a tape recording of different languages and music
pictures of people from around the world
coins from different countries
pictures of inventions such as cars, planes and spacecraft
a plan of our solar system
dried foods
information about Earth time and an old clock or watch

What else would you send into space? Is there one thing that would represent Earth and its people?
Remember that aliens won't understand your language.

2 Collect together all the things on your list. Make the collection as light and compact as possible – remember that it has to fit into a small capsule on board a space probe!

3 Glue some paper around the tin to cover the labels. Design lots of signs and symbols to draw on your capsule. They could be about Earth and its people. Try to devise a symbol to show how to play a cassette tape.

Space Travel Through the Ages

1944
The V2 (left) was a German rocket developed near the end of World War II to attack southern England. After the war many of the scientists who worked on the V2 went to the USA. They used the knowledge gained from building the V2 to begin the American rocket programme.

1950s
During the 1950s Britain developed the successful Blue Streak rocket. It was originally designed to be a missile, but in the 1960s it was used as part of the Europa rocket. Unfortunately, the Europa project ran out of money and never launched a satellite. However, much of the technology has been used for the ESA Ariane rocket programme (right).

1961
Soviet cosmonaut Yuri Gagarin made history by being the first man to fly into Earth orbit. His spacecraft was *Vostok 1* (above). The whole mission lasted just 108 minutes.

1967
A month before *Apollo 1* was due to take off, three astronauts were inside the capsule carrying out routine tests. A fire swept through the cabin and all three died. An enquiry found faults in the spacecraft design and the *Apollo* programme was delayed by a year and a half.

1967
Soviet cosmonaut Vladimir Komarov was killed when the parachutes on his *Soyuz I* spacecraft failed to open as it returned to Earth.

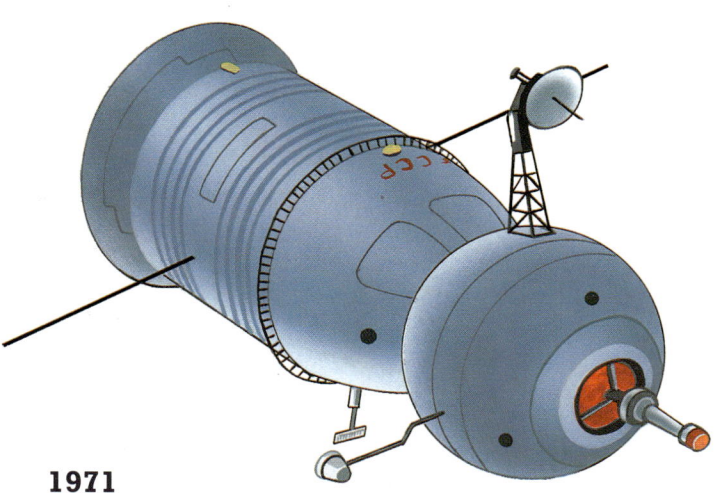

1971
Disaster struck the *Soyuz* programme again in 1971. Three crew members were nearing the end of their 24-day stay on the space station *Salyut 1* (above). The procedure for returning to Earth was going smoothly when an air valve jerked open. The air inside the *Soyuz II* spacecraft was lost and the cosmonauts suffocated.

1986
Just 73 seconds after blast-off, the shuttle *Challenger* exploded. All seven crew members were killed. The disaster was watched by millions of people on live television. It was found that one of the booster rockets had leaked, causing the main fuel tank to explode. The shuttle programme was delayed by two years while the booster was re-designed.

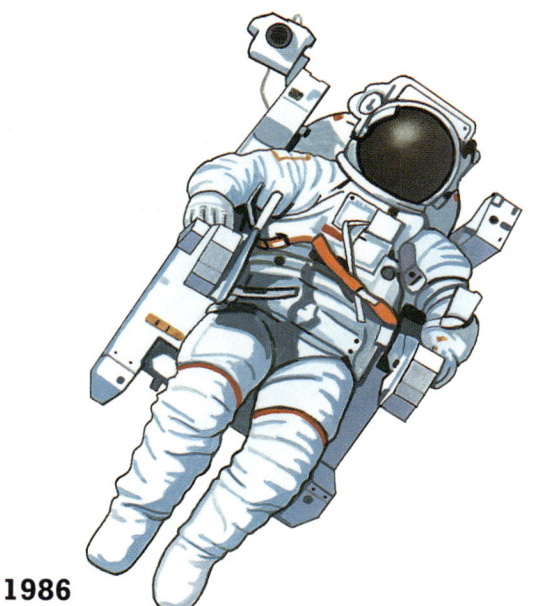

1986
American astronaut Bruce McCandless made the first space walk (above) using a Manned Manoeuvring Unit (MMU). The MMU is a backpack worn by astronauts which lets them work freely in space without being connected to their spacecraft.

1989
The *Galileo* space probe was launched. When it eventually reaches Jupiter, it will study the planet for two years.

1990
The Hubble Space Telescope (above) was sent into orbit. Photographs taken using this telescope are so much clearer as it is able to see seven times further into space than other telescopes. However, the first pictures sent back indicated that there was a problem with the telescope which would require astronauts being sent into space to repair it.

Glossary

Asteroid a small object that orbits around the Sun.

Astronaut someone who is trained to travel in space.

Atmosphere the layer of gases that surround the Earth or other planets.

Capsule a self-contained spacecraft, or part of one.

Comet a small member of the solar system which shines as it nears the Sun.

Cosmonaut the Russian word for astronaut.

Crater a hole made when a rock from outer space dents the surface of a planet or a moon.

Earth the third planet from the Sun.

E.S.A. the European Space Agency.

Gravity the pull of the Earth on everything on it or near it in space.

Launch To take off from land into space.

Lunar belonging to a moon.

Manned operated by people.

Mission a space flight.

Module a self-contained unit forming part of a spacecraft.

Moon a satellite.

Moon base a station or headquarters from which activities take place on the moon.

Orbit the path taken when one body circles around another in space.

Parachute Apparatus used for slowing down the landing of a spacecraft.

Planet a large body that orbits the sun.

Probe A spacecraft that is launched into space to explore planets and other bodies.

Rocket a fast and powerful engine.

Satellite a small body that orbits a larger one in space. Can be natural (Earth's moon) or man-made.

Solar power energy from the Sun.

Solar system the Sun and all its planets including moons and asteroids, metors and comets.

Space-suit the protective outfit worn by astronauts.

Weightlessness the condition experienced by astronauts in orbit when they seem to have no weight.

RESOURCES

Books to read

The Newsround Book of Space by N. Heathcote, M Corwin and S. Staples (BBC Books)

Space Exploration by J. Davies (Chambers)

The Encyclopedia of U.S. Spacecraft by B. Yenne (Hamlyn/Bison)

The Children's Space Atlas by R. Kerrod (Apple Press)

The Picture World of Space Voyages by Norman Barret (Franklin Watts, 1990)

The Picture World of Astronauts by Norman Barrett (Franklin Watts, 1990)

The Picture World of Rockets and Satellites by Norman Barrett (Franklin Watts, 1990)

The Picture World of Space Shuttles by Norman Barrett (Franklin Watts, 1990)

Windows on the World: Space by Sue Becklake (Dorling Kindersley, 1990)

Space Library series by Gregory Vogt (Franklin Watts, 1990)

Places to visit

The Science Museum
Exhibition Road
South Kensington
London, SW7 2DD
Tel: 071-938 8000

Space Expo
Keplerplaan 3
2201 AZ Noordwijk
The Netherlands
Tel: (1719) 46460

Spaceport USA
Kennedy Space Centre
Florida 32899
United States
Tel: (407) 867 2363

Jodrell Bank Observatory
Cheshire
England

The London Planetarium,
Marylebone Road,
London

Computer Games

There are several "Space simulation" games available. These include an exciting game based on the space shuttle, available for most formats.

INDEX

Aldrin, Edwin 12
Apollo 5, 12, 13, 29
Ariane 4, 28
Armstrong, Neil 12
Atlantis 4

Blue Streak 28
Buran 4

Challenger 16, 29
China 25
Collins, Michael 12
Columbia 4, 17
cosmonauts 4

Discovery 4

Endeavour 4
European Space Agency (ESA) 4, 9, 21, 23, 30
Europa 26

Freedom 21

Gagarin, Yuri 5, 28
Galileo 29
Giotto 9

Halley's comet 9
Hubble Space Telescope 29

India 24
Irwin, James 13
Israel 24

Japan 25
Jupiter 5, 8, 9, 26, 29

Komarov, Vladimir 29

Luna 3 8
Lunar Roving Vehicle 13

Manned Maneuvering Unit (MMU) 29
Mariner 2 8
Mariner 4 8
Mariner 10 8

Mars 8
McCandless, Bruce 29
Mercury 8
Mir 4, 24
Moon 8, 9, 12, 13, 14, 15, 30

National Aeronautics and Space Administration (NASA) 16, 21
Neptune 8, 9

Pioneer 10 5, 8, 26
Pioneer 11 8
Pluto 8
probes 5, 8, 9, 10, 11, 30

rockets 4, 5, 6, 24, 28, 30

Salyut 1 20, 21, 29
satellites 11, 24, 30
Saturn 8, 9
Saturn V 5, 12
Scott, David 13
Sharman, Helen 24
Skylab 5, 20, 21
Soyuz 24, 29
space shuttle 4, 16, 17, 18, 19, 24, 25
space stations 4, 5, 20, 21, 22, 23

Tereshkova, Valentina 5

Uranus 8, 9

V2 28
Venera 7 8
Venus 8
Viking 8
Vostok 1 5, 6, 28
Vostok 6 5
Voyager 1 9, 26
Voyager 2 8, 9

Additional photographs:
NASA/Science Photo Library 8, 17, 26